WAYS TO GIVE CHILDREN

at

HOME
WORK
AND
PLAY

Dr. Cindy Iannarelli
Business Cents Resources

Honey Money Lyrics and Music by Mikki Matthews

Business Cents, Bizbee, Business Can Bee Fun, and Honey Money are trademarks of Business Cents Resources.

Special discounts on bulk quantities are available to corporations, professional associations, and other organizations.

Contact:

BUSINESS CENTS RESOURCES
3038 Washington Pike
Bridgeville, PA 15017
1-800-67-CINDY or (412) 221-8924
Fax (412) 221-0150
Or visit us at WWW.DRCINDY.COM

Library of Congress Cataloging-in-Publication Number 98-93257

Iannarelli, Cindy.
    101 ways to give children business cents : at home, work and play / Cindy Iannarelli. -- 1st ed.
    p. cm.
    Includes index.
    ISBN: 1-889107-01-8

    1. Children--Finance, Personal. 2. Child rearing.
3. Business education. I. Title. II. Title: One hundred one ways to give children business cents. III. Title: One hundred and one ways to give children business cents

HQ784.S4I36 1998   649'.16
                           QBI98-829

*Dedicated to my son
Joncarlo,
his triplet cousins
Brianna, Carina, Domenique
and older sister Alexandria,
and the next generation
growing up in families
around the world.*

CONTENTS

BUSINESS CENTS ACTIVITY #

1. Building a Business District
2. Checkbook Balancer
3. Television Teasers
4. Budget Blast
5. Packages Promotions
6. Classified Ads
7. Yellow Pages
8. My Turn Menu
9. Hire Out
10. Message Light
11. Sunday Newspaper
12. A Day Ahead
13. Invest Your Nest
14. Why Not
15. Sibling Assignments
16. Home Page Happenings

17. Crazy Coupons
18. Product Makers
19. Create a Product
20. Volunteer Visitors
21. Kitchen Gadgets
22. Room to Move
23. Treasure Hunt
24. Agreements to Keep
25. Recall Ad
26. Create a Campaign
27. Sure Security
28. Purely Profits
29. Need to Negotiate
30. Home Repair
31. Mailing Mania

CHAPTER 2 - BUSINESS CENTS AT WORK........Page 33

BUSINESS CENTS ACTIVITY #

CHAPTER 3 – BUSINESS CENTS AT PLAY ....Page 63

BUSINESS CENTS ACTIVITY #

61. Time Trade-Off
62. Exchange Game
63. Map Mania
64. Itinerary Building
65. Travel Budgeting
66. Wardrobe Wizard
67. Reservations Confirmed
68. Time Zones
69. Safety Shipping
70. Travel Log
71. Billboards Galore
72. Observe Your World
73. Gross Volume
74. Make the Product
75. Event Expenses
76. Lessons at Lessons
77. Jingle Jangle
78. Radio Whamo
79. Barbie the Business Owner
80. Reading Record
81. Volunteer Values

82. Promo Promotions
83. Companion Sales
84. Bankrupt Dreams
85. Organizational Chart
86. Book Businesses
87. Collectible Catch
88. Pet Schedule
89. Play Around
90. Weekend at Grandpa's
91. Rate the Business
92. Price Value
93. Signs to Find
94. Fun Freebies
95. Customers are Right
96. Sell, Sell, Sell
97. The BIG Purchase
98. Auction Action
99. Bank Around
100. Team Purchase
101. Change Back

Bizbee Says:

How Good is Your Business Cents?

INTRODUCTION TO
THE BUSINESS CENTS METHOD

This book may be your first introduction to the Business Cents Method of teaching children business skills. The Business Cents Method has developed out of almost two decades of research and hands-on practical experience in business. It is the first of its kind to blend skill and attitude development for children as young as three years old.

Every child, regardless of economic background, can build their business cents over time through a series of interactive activities described here. These activities simulate real-world business experiences. Children learn the 24 BUSINESS CENTS SKILLS which are categorized into 5 skill groups.

BUSINESS CENTS SKILLS development starts at age three and continues into one's adult life. The chart on page iii describes your role at each of the five stages. Research shows children can benefit by being exposed to introductory business concepts in their early years. Hands-on activities during the pre-teen and teen years add to their learning. Broadening experiences such as college, internships, and work abroad add to their experiences prior to making a formal entry into an organization. Lastly we encourage putting their "business cents" to good use in leadership roles in their workplaces, families, and communities.

The BUSINESS CENTS mascot, BIZBEE, the business bee, makes business fun for the younger set. Follow him, and your children are sure to find sweet success in life. No matter what career your children select BUSINESS CENTS will serve them well. They will be better consumers and employees and will better manage their money and the people around them. These skills will lead them to more rewarding and satisfying lives.

HOW TO USE THIS BOOK

This book was designed so parents, grandparents and caregivers could easily work these activities into your daily lives. Educators can use the book to bring more excitement and real-world activities into the classroom. The BUSINESS CENTS CURRICULUM BOOKS provided these skills in ready-to-use classroom format.

Each activity identifies the primary BUSINESS CENTS skill which the children learn. Each activity also reinforces additional skills. An estimated time period and age range is provided. The younger children need your supervision and their activities should be limited to short time periods. While the older children can work on their own research shows they perfer to spend time with their parents. Use these activities to build quality family time together.

Keep this book handy to refer to over and over again. With more resources now available such as computers, the internet, and books, be sure to use them to your advantage to continue to give business cents to the next generation.

Be sure to look for updates on our web site:

www.DRCINDY.com

Let us hear how you improved the
BUSINESS CENTS
in your family.

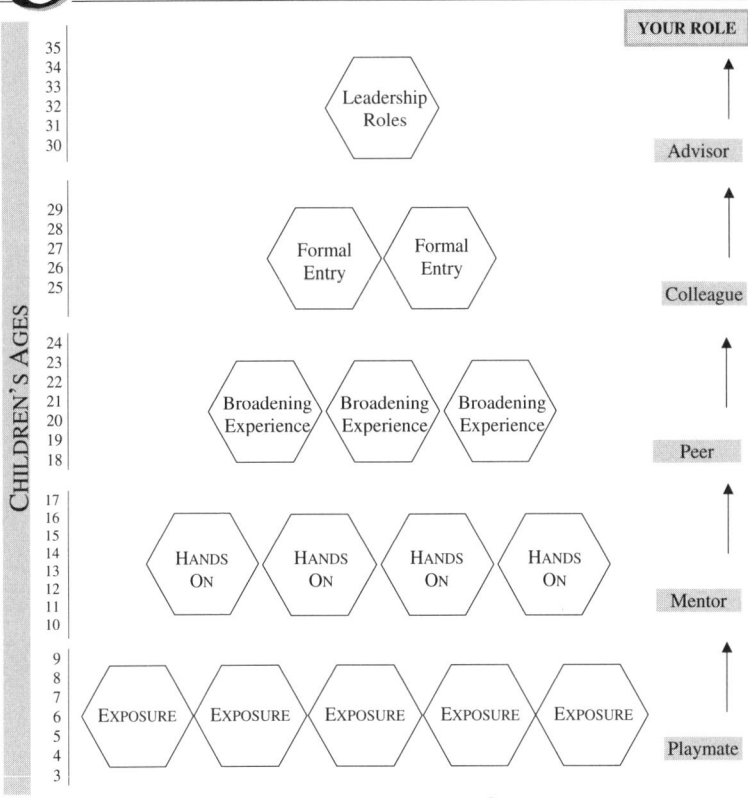

5 STAGES TO TRAINING AND DEVELOPING CHILDREN IN BUSINESS
THE FOUNDATION FOR A SUCCESSFUL CAREER

24
Business Cents
Skills Every Child
Should Know

I. Self-Starting Skills
1. *Initiating*
2. *Researching*
3. *Planning*
4. *Implementing*

II. People Skills
5. *Hiring*
6. *Teambuilding*
7. *Leading*
8. *Evaluating*

III. Marketing Skills
9. *Communicating*
10. *Satisfying Customers*
11. *Advertising*
12. *Promoting*
13. *Selling*
14. *Presenting*

IV. Money Skills
15. *Analyzing*
16. *Purchasing*
17. *Accounting*
18. *Financing*
19. *Profiting*
20. *Investing*

V. Leadership Skills
21. *Negotiating*
22. *Decision-Making*
23. *Organizing*
24. *Managing*

Business Cents  At Home

When my mother opened her own business my father offered to take over the household grocery shopping. The deal he made with my brother and me was that if we cut coupons, organized them, and selected the products on each shopping trip the savings would go into a special jar. As the jar filled up, we could decide how to spend the money. I remember trips to the amusement park, special dinners, and purchases for the family that were a real treat.

Chapter 1

BUILDING A BUSINESS DISTRICT
BUSINESS CENTS SKILL #3 PLANNING

ACTIVITY:

Let children wrap each box, which will represent a business. They can decorate the outside and add signs, hours of operation and window displays.

- Put several boxes together and create your own shopping mall or business district.
- Work as a team and create a city together.

Bizbee Says:

Own a Special Events Company

MATERIALS:

- Cereal or cracker boxes
- Tissue or brown wrapping paper
- Tape
- Markers or Crayons

AGES: 3-12 **TIME**: 15-45 Min

CHECKBOOK BALANCER
BUSINESS CENTS SKILL #17 ACCOUNTING

ACTIVITY:

Let children be a part of your household routine to pay the bills.

- They can open envelopes and find the amount due.
- They can double check the dates of service or purchases made.
- They can write out the checks or enter them into the computer or pay by phone.
- They can reconcile the checks each month with the bank statement and put the checks in numerical order.

MATERIALS:

- Bills
- Bank statements

Dr. Cindy Says:

The Business Cents Method is based upon repetition of these tasks. Get in the habit of doing them over and over again with your children.

AGES: 6-18   **TIME:** 30+ min.

TELEVISION TEASERS
BUSINESS CENTS SKILL #13 SELLING

ACTIVITY:

As you watch television together, take notice of the commercials. Ask your children:

- What are they really selling? (e.g. Looking good, being socially acceptable, making friends)

- To keep a small notebook by the television to make a list of which companies are advertising on each show.

- Why are these types of companies selecting certain shows?

- To make a list of the other shows where they could also advertise to reach the same market.

Bizbee Says: See who can do this for the most shows each week and come up with a prize (being excused from a chore).

Own a Publishing Company

MATERIALS:

- Television
- Notebook

AGES: 6-18

TIME: 10+ min. per commercial

BUDGET BLAST
BUSINESS CENTS SKILL #15 ANALYZING

ACTIVITY:

Work with the children to make a household budget for each month.

- They can use your check register as a guide and anticipate seasonal fluctuations.

- After a few months make the process into a game by having them estimate the amounts due and then compare them against the actuals.

- Carry the process out throughout the year by keeping track each month of who is the closest. Work up to a big prize (having a slumber party, selecting a family outing, staying up late for the holidays).

- Consider computer programs for the process.

MATERIALS:
- Check Register

AGES: 7-18

TIME: 60 min. per month

Hear the BUZZ

One dad responded to his son's request for a new swing set, "I'll have to go to work and make more money before we can get it." When the father returned home that evening, the son asked, "Dad, do we have enough money yet?"

PACKAGE PROMOTIONS
BUSINESS CENTS SKILL #12 PROMOTIONS

5

ACTIVITY:

Tell each child to find ten product packages throughout the house.

Look at each one and:

- Identify the first thing you notice.

- Make a list of five types of information found on every package.

- Make a list of the two main colors used in each one.

- Make a new design for the package.

Bizbee Says:

Bee a Self-Employed Photographer

MATERIALS:

- Household Product Packages

- Paper

- Markers, crayons or paint

AGES: 3-18 **TIME:** 30+ Min.

CLASSIFIED ADS
BUSINESS CENTS SKILL #9 COMMUNICATING

ACTIVITY:

Look in the Classified advertising section of a Sunday paper or those in the back of magazines.

- Have each child identify something they are interested in.
- Make a list of questions they would like to know about the item in the ad.
- Call and make an inquiry about those items.
- Repeat the process for similar items and then compare the results
- Write a classified ad for one household item.
- Calculate how much the ad would cost by following the published rate card or calling to get rate information.

MATERIALS:
- Newspaper Classified Section
- Magazine Classified Section

AGES: 7-18

TIME: 15+ min. per ad

Dr. Cindy Says:

Bee sure to say "thanks for helping," "good job," or "good thinking" to your child on a regular basis after engaging in these activities.

YELLOW PAGES
BUSINESS CENTS SKILL #11 ADVERTISING

7

ACTIVITY:

Let the children look up one of their favorite stores or services in the yellow pages.

- Do the competitors have an advertisement? If so, how large is it?
- Make a list of all of the competitors.
- Do they have an advertisement?
- Which advertisement is the most eye catching?
- Read the names of three businesses and their phone numbers. Which one do you remember?
- Design a new advertisement for a business.

Bizbee Says:

Own a Restaurant

MATERIALS:

- Yellow Pages
- Paper
- Pencils, markers or crayons

AGES: 7-18 **TIME:** 20+ min.

AGES: 3-6 Select their favorite graphics in an ad.

MY TURN MENU

BUSINESS CENTS SKILL #23 ORGANIZING

ACTIVITY:

Have each child plan a menu for one meal for the household.

- Make a list of ingredients.

- Prepare a budget for money and preparation time.

- Actually select the items and compare the prices.

- Determine how much each meal would be if you were preparing for 50.

- Write a work schedule and process for making 50 meals.

AGES: 9-18
TIME: 100 min.

AGES: 3-8 Can work on making just one item. (Example: How many cookies come from one batch?)

Hear the "BUZZ"

A five-year-old accompanied her mother to her New York show room which featured expensive china and giftware. Under the spotlights and the glamour of Fifth Avenue, the child replied, "Wow Mom, why didn't you tell me about this place before?

HIRE OUT
BUSINESS CENTS SKILL #16 PURCHASING

9

ACTIVITY:

Let the children make a dinner choice on take-out night.

- Which option is the best value?
- Have them make a list of the order and phone or fax it to the restaurant.
- How is the meal presented? Is it packaged correctly? Is it hot? Was it correct? Would you order from them again?
- How would you describe the meal to a friend?

Bizbee Says:

Own a Medical Software Company

MATERIALS:

- Take-out Menus

AGES: 7-18   **TIME:** 15 min.

MESSAGE LIGHT
BUSINESS CENTS SKILL #9 COMMUNICATING

ACTIVITY:

Create a new voice mail message each month for the household telephone.
- Write down what you intend to say and practice prior to recording.
- Call area businesses after hours to hear their recorded messages.
- Write down new messages for these businesses and practice out loud.

Dr. Cindy Says:

AGES: 7-10

TIME: 15 minutes

BEE sure to give each child a similar experience. These exercises are just as important for girls as they are for boys.

AGES: 4-6 Can listen and practice a greeting with their name.

SUNDAY NEWSPAPER
BUSINESS CENTS SKILL #3 PLANNING

11

ACTIVITY:

Go through the paper for advertisements.

- Cut out everything you would need if you were setting up an office.
- Make a game by seeing who can find the most items in a given time.
- Add up the prices and see how much the office would cost. Which child would have the least expensive office?
- Arrange the items on a piece of cardboard to look like the office.

Bizbee Says:

Make Novelties

MATERIALS:

- Newspaper
- Scissors
- Glue
- Cardboard

AGES: 5-14   **TIME:** 20+ min.

A DAY AHEAD
BUSINESS CENTS SKILL #23 ORGANIZING

ACTIVITY:

Encourage children to think about the next day's activities and:

- Select something from the closet to wear.

- Make sure it is not wrinkled and does not need to be mended.

- Select all items needed to go with it (underwear, socks, jewelry, shoes).

- Put them all in one place.

- Place all other items nearby such as books, gym bag, etc.

- Enjoy how quickly you can get dressed and out the door in the mornings!

Dr. Cindy Says:

Keep a Business Cents notebook with your activities in it.
Add to it year after year.

AGES: 6-18

TIME: 10+ minutes

INVEST YOUR NEST
BUSINESS CENTS SKILL #20 INVESTING

13

ACTIVITY:

Encourage children to gather up the money they may have in the house and:

- Call area banks or look up their savings rates on the internet.
- Open a savings account and commit to making deposits on a regular basis (weekly/monthly).
- Ask the bank manager to explain how their money will earn interest in the bank.

- Set a goal such as a house, college, new bike, piano lessons or a business to keep saving for.
- Keep a picture of the goal where you can see it everyday.

Bizbee Says:

Own a Medical Office

AGES: 6-18 **TIME:** 15+ min.

AGES: 3-6 use a bank at home.

SHOEBOX FILING
BUSINESS CENTS SKILL #23 ORGANIZING

14

ACTIVITY:

Identify projects around the household where children can help you to stay organized.

- Give them shoe boxes which they can cover and label.
- Discuss a system of organization and let them carry it out (buttons, craft supplies, photos, wrapping paper, etc.)
- Older children can also do filing and more detailed organizing.
- Offer a reward for a complete and neat job when finished (they can go to that sporting event, have friends over, eat their favorite meal...)

MATERIALS:
- Shoeboxes
- File folders
- Wrapping paper
- Labels

AGES: 7-18   **TIME:** 20+ min.

AGES: 3-6 try this activity with their toys.

Dr. Cindy Says:

Use Bizbee's honey factory to teach your child. Bees work as a team, we follow a leader (the queen), we are always searching for materials(flowers), and our wax and honey products have hundreds of uses. How many can you name?

SIBLING ASSIGNMENTS
BUSINESS CENTS SKILL #6 TEAMBUILDING

15

ACTIVITY:

Give siblings or cousins assignments to do together. Have them begin by taking time to plan who is going to do each part. After the project, discuss what actually happened and what they would do differently the next time. Projects include:

- Cleaning out the garage
- Baking cookies
- Running a lemonade stand
- Yard work
- Planning a vacation or outing

Bizbee Says:

AGES: 8-18
TIME: 15 min. for planning and debriefing

AGES: 3-7 Be the organizer and go through the same process

Own a Limosine Company

HOME PAGE HAPPENINGS
BUSINESS CENTS SKILL #7 SUPERVISING

ACTIVITY:

Encourage children to work together to create a home page just for your family. Go to the library and scan the internet for ideas.

- What activities should be included?
- What graphics should be used?
- Design the layout for each on paper.
- Have the children take turns being the supervisor of the project.
- Expand by making a home page for your school, church, community.

AGES: 8-18

TIME: 30 minutes

Dr. Cindy Says:

Make Business Cents common sense in your family by getting everyone involved in the process.

CRAZY COUPONS
BUSINESS CENTS SKILL #23 ORGANIZING

17

ACTIVITY:

Guide the children to collect coupons from magazines, newspapers, and internet ads. Take them on a visit to your regular grocery store and observe the items in each row.

- Make an envelope for each row.
- Organize the coupons in the order you would see the products.
- When it is time to shop, make a shopping list and put the items in the order you will see them.
- Pull out the coupons which correspond to the products needed.
- Match the products and the coupons when shopping.

Bizbee Says:

Bee a Self-Employed Instructor

MATERIALS:
- Envelopes
- Newspapers
- Magazines

AGES: 7-10   **TIME:** 40 min.

AGES: 3-6 can help in the cutting process and the matching process

PRODUCT MAKERS
BUSINESS CENTS SKILL #2 RESEARCH

ACTIVITY:

Let the children go through your household and find ten products with a label on it.

- Identify who manufactured the product and where they are located.
- Use the internet and phone directories to get the complete information.
- Write a letter about something you like or dislike about the product or their advertising campaign.
- Mail, fax or e-mail
- Collect the responses and compare them.

MATERIALS:

- Writing paper
- Stamps
- Envelopes

AGES: 7-18   **TIME:** 40 min.

Dr. Cindy Says:

Many wealthy people today have their own business. They start with an idea and keep working at it. Sometimes it takes 10 to 20 years but someone has to start.

CREATE A PRODUCT
BUSINESS CENTS SKILL #1 INITIATING

19

ACTIVITY:

Let the children locate a product in your household that is widely advertised.

- Design a new name for the product which sounds similar.
- Design a new package which looks similar.
- Design a new advertising which has the same message

(EXAMPLE: Captain Crunch can become Captain Scrunch)

Bizbee Says:

Own a
Talent Agency

AGES: 5-18

TIME: 30 minutes

VOLUNTEER VISITORS
BUSINESS CENTS SKILL #14 PRESENTING

20

ACTIVITY:

Take the children to make a visit to a local senior citizens center or retirement home. Have them call to make arrangements with the activity coordinator.

- Prepare a presentation (sing a song, read a homework assignment, do a dance).
- Practice standing in front of a mirror and introducing yourself, saying your name, age, grade, and your hobbies.
- Coordinate an outfit with the presentation.
- Make something to give to all of the attendees.

MATERIALS:

- Supplies necessary to make items to pass out.

AGES: 5-18

TIME: 60 minutes prep.

Dr. Cindy Says:

Keep a chart listing the five Business Cents skill groups and the days of the week. Have your child put a star on when they practice each skill. Offer a special reward when they have so many.

KITCHEN GADGETS
BUSINESS CENTS SKILL #1 INITIATING

21

ACTIVITY:

Let the children go through the kitchen and identify five objects.

- Ask them to write down 3 other ways each product could be used if living on another planet.
- Have each child do individually and then compare what they came up with.
- Let them also work on some items together.

Bizbee Says:

Own a Family Fun Center

AGES: 5-18

TIME: 30 minutes

ROOM TO MOVE
Business Cents Skill #1 Initiating

22

ACTIVITY:

Assume your household is getting crowded. Have the children go through and select one item they would sell. Write up a work sheet with the following answers:

- How would they sell it?
- Where would they sell it?
- Write what they would tell a prospective buyer.
- How much would they sell it for?
- How much would it cost them to sell it?
- If it is something you really would not mind selling, let them put their plan into action. Work out a commission for their efforts.

AGES: 7-18

TIME: 30 minutes

Dr. Cindy Says:

Business owners can take these activities and make them even more specific to their business situation.

TREASURE HUNT
BUSINESS CENTS SKILL #2 RESEARCHING

23

ACTIVITY:

Give your children fifteen minutes to go through the house and find as many things as they can that have something to do with business. (Clue: advertisements, packaging, direct mail, bills).

Discuss their business treasures as a group and ask them:

- How is this item related to business?
- What company is it from?
- How could you improve it?
- Where did you find it?

Bizbee Says:

Bee a Self-Employed Physical Therapist

Reverse the game the next time and give them a list of items and see who is the fastest in locating them.

MATERIALS:

- Business items in easy reach.

AGES: 5-18   **TIME:** 30 min.

AGREEMENTS TO KEEP
BUSINESS CENTS SKILL #9 NEGOTIATING

24

ACTIVITY:

Write down every agreement you make with your children or that they make among themselves.

- Include the date and exactly what each party has agreed to do.
- Include the time period that the agreement is valid.
- Include the consequences if broken.
- Post on the refrigerator or a bulletin board or keep in a notebook.

Dr. Cindy Says:

When you relate business skills to everyday life, children take a greater interest and they learn without even realizing it.

MATERIALS:

- Notebook

AGES: 7-18   **TIME:** 15 min.

RECALL AD
BUSINESS CENTS SKILL #11 ADVERTISING

25

ACTIVITY:

Ask your children what their favorite advertisement is.

- What do they like about it?
- Why is it their favorite?
- What do they remember about it?
- What do the other family members think about it?
- Which ad do they like least?

Bizbee Says:

Own a Laboratory

AGES: 3-18

TIME: 5 minutes

CREATE A CAMPAIGN
BUSINESS CENTS SKILL #13 SELLING

26

ACTIVITY:

Tell your child to pick an item of clothing they are wearing.

- What would you say if you were trying to sell it to someone?
- Design an advertisement for the item.
- What type of promotion would you design to sell more of the item?

AGES: 5-18

TIME: 10 minutes

Dr. Cindy Says:

The fifty/fifty rule works well for children ages 3 to 43. When children want an expensive item, they have to earn 50%. This rule even applies to trust funds where children are only entitled to the same amount as their paycheck.

SURE SECURITY
BUSINESS CENTS SKILL #4 IMPLEMENTING

27

ACTIVITY:

Let the children design or redesign a security system for the household.

- Where should the smoke detectors go?
- How can we remember to change the batteries?
- What emergency numbers should we have listed?
- Where should we keep the numbers?
- Are the doors and windows secure?

- Write down emergency procedures in case of fire, theft, injury.
- How do we protect ourselves outside of the household?

Bizbee Says:

*Own a
Retail Store*

AGES: 3-18

TIME: 40 minutes

PURLEY PROFITS
BUSINESS CENTS SKILL #19 PROFITING

28

ACTIVITY:

Let your children keep track of your charge card expenditures.

- Have them keep the receipts in a special envelope at home.
- When the statement comes in, let them compare the receipts with the purchases.
- Let them see how you profit by adding up the frequent flyer miles, or cash back incentives by using your card.
- Discuss the cost of not paying off the balance each month.

AGES: 7-18

TIME: 20 minutes

Dr. Cindy Says:

Keeping their room clean and basic family chores which are expected of each family member should not be paid for with an allowance. These chores are expected for the basic food, shelter, and clothing.

NEED TO NEGIOTIATE
BUSINESS CENTS SKILL #21 NEGOTIATING

ACTIVITY:

The next time your child asks for something, be more conscious about turning the negotiating process into an exercise.

- With every request, ask them for three reasons why they are deserving of it.
- Ask them for all of the facts.
- If they are not deserving at the moment, ask them what they promise to do in exchange.

Bizbee Says:

- Have them put their request in writing for big items.

Uniforms

Make Uniforms

AGES: 4-18

TIME: 5 minutes

HOME REPAIR
BUSINESS CENTS SKILL #4 IMPLEMENTING

30

ACTIVITY:

Let the children make a list of things around the house which are in need of repair.

- List the item and the repair needed (include small items and large items such as paint jobs, roof, cars, etc.)
- Let the children estimate how long the repair would take and how much it would be to fix it.
- They can visit hardware stores or call businesses to try to get this information.
- Make a schedule and prioritize which repairs would be made first.
- Let the children be involved with the actual repair when possible.

AGES: 8-18

TIME: 15 + min per item

AGES: 3-7 can help with small jobs.

Dr. Cindy Says:

Allowance should be given for the extras. One rule which some families use is children are able to earn up to their age each week. Often parents have another rule, which is at least 20% of it has to go into savings and 20% to charity.

MAILING MANIA
BUSINESS CENTS SKILL #6 TEAMBUILDING

31

ACTIVITY:

Let the children open and sort the mail with you.

- Put the bills, personal letters, and advertisements in separate piles.
- Let them seal and stamp envelopes that you are mailing.
- Let them prepare their own birthday invitations.
- In a business setting, they can often sort, count and affix labels.

Bizbee Says:

Own a
Resale Shop

AGES: 3-18

TIME: 10 minutes

  **Business Cents** **At Work**

Once a week after school my father would pick me up and we would go to his laundromat to empty the money from the machines. Each week I would count quarter after quarter. Finally I said, "Dad, how can you stand to count all of these quarters week after week?" He replied, "Cin, as long as they are my quarters I can count them all day."

Chapter 2

WRAP IT UP
BUSINESS CENTS SKILL #15 ANALYZING

32

ACTIVITY:

Encourage the children to make their own wrapping paper for all family gifts.

- Start with plain tissue paper (it comes in many colors).
- Let them add their own paint, markers, stickers, and stamp designs.
- Let dry before using or storing.
- This is a great rainy day activity.
- Have the children add up the cost of the paper and the art materials.
- Let them compare the cost with that of prepackaged wrapping paper.
- Let the children calculate the savings.

MATERIALS:
- Tissue Paper
- Art Supplies

Dr. Cindy Says:

A good business sense is an asset in the job market.

AGES: 3-12   **TIME:** 15 min.

LABEL FOR STICKING
BUSINESS CENTS SKILL #23 ORGANIZING

33

ACTIVITY:

Identify items which need to be labeled. These can be:

- File folders at work
- Storage bins
- Supply shelves
- Toy containers and items at home

Have the children write the labels first to check for spelling and neatness (they can write them or do them on the computer).

Bizbee Says:

Own a Technical School

MATERIALS:

- Labels
- Markers
- Computer (Optional)

AGES: 7-18 **TIME:** 20+ min.

SHORT STOPS
BUSINESS CENTS SKILL #14 PRESENTING

ACTIVITY:

Take your children along when doing short errands for home or work.

- Explain who they will be visiting.
- Talk about the expected behavior.
- Teach them to extend their hand and give a firm hand shake.
- Have them say, "My name is..."
- Look the other person in the eye.
- Listen and answer questions.
- Introduce them as your assistant.

AGES:　3-9
TIME:　5+ min.

AGES:　10-18
TIME:　10+ min.

Dr. Cindy Says:

Just like learning to play sports or musical instruments, business skills are much easier to learn when young.

CHECKS AND BALANCES
BUSINESS CENTS SKILL #18 FINANCING

35

ACTIVITY:

Give your children an appreciation of how money comes in and out of a business or a household.

- Show a bank statement and let them find the deposits
- Let them match the checks to the bank statement
- Put the checks in order
- Add up the deposits and subtract the checks

Bizbee Says:

SPORTS BROADCASTING CENTER

SPORTS NEWS

Bee a Self-Employed Announcer

MATERIALS:

- Bank Statements

AGES: 7-18   TIME: 20+ min.

SSS (Sorting, Stocking & Straightening)
BUSINESS CENTS SKILL #8 EVALUATING

36

ACTIVITY:

Give each child an assignment of
sorting, stocking, or straightening.
NOTE: This could be in a retail setting or in an office
with bags of change, a desk drawer, or supply cabinet.

- Let them observe the before and after.
- Have them evaluate the job they did and that of another person.
- Could it still be improved?
- If so, how?
- How long did it take? Who was the most efficient?
- What could they do differently the next time?

Dr. Cindy Says:

You can't
loose by giving
your child
business sense.
It is a wise
investment in
the future.

AGES: 4-18

TIME: 20+ minutes

ON THE MOVE
BUSINESS CENTS SKILL #9 COMMUNICATING

37

ACTIVITY:

Let your child find an item you may be looking to purchase. Have children:

- Call various stores to locate.
- Identify the price and which is the best value.
- Get directions if a retail location.
- Write up a report for you.
- Use as an exercise to find obscure items and see how good they are at getting people to help them along the way.

Bizbee Says:

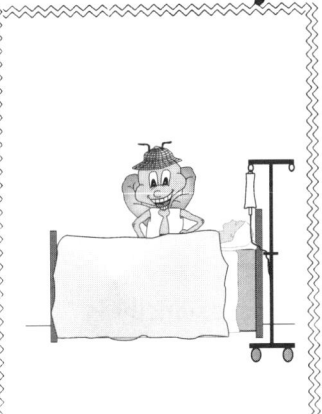

Own a
Personal Care Home

AGES: 7-18

TIME: 30+ minutes

PUTTING IT ALL TOGETHER
BUSINESS CENTS SKILL #24 MANAGING

38

ACTIVITY:

Identify opportunities in your business or community for your children to work on a piecework project.

- Many assembly shops have piecework jobs which can be completed at home.
- The rate of pay is usually by the piece.
- Piecework can include computer components, craft items, specialty baskets, booklets, mailers, printers.
- Look in your local paper or call area businesses.
- Let children commit to several hours or piecework a week.
- For bigger jobs, let teenagers organize their friends.

AGES: 12-18

TIME: Per project

Dr. Cindy Says:

Research shows that when it comes to giving children business sense, doing these exercises regularly is better than occasionally, but occasionally is better than nothing.

OFFICE OBSERVATION
BUSINESS CENTS SKILL #22 Decision Making

39

ACTIVITY:

Include your children in meetings with advisors, people you may be purchasing from and family board meetings.

- Let them listen and see how decisions are made.
- Have them write a summary of the meeting.
- Ask them for their "read" on the players.
- Is what they were saying what they really felt?

Bizbee Says:

AGES: 8-13
TIME: 20 minutes

AGES: 14-18
TIME: 60 minutes

*Own a
Monogram Shop*

COMPETITOR CHASE
BUSINESS CENTS SKILL #2 RESEARCHING

40

ACTIVITY:

Let your children develop a list of competitors of the business where you or a family member is employed.

- Use the internet and library sources.
- If customers are not buying a product or service from this business, where else could they satisfy their needs.
- Look up the listing in the yellow pages and take note of what competitors are advertising there.

Dr. Cindy Says:

Research shows children look to their parents for advice and career direction.

MATERIALS:

- Internet
- Yellow Pages

AGES: 8-18   **TIME:** 45+ min.

JOB DESCRIPTIONS
BUSINESS CENTS SKILL #5 HIRING

41

ACTIVITY:

Encourage the children to think about describing the jobs people and things do.

- Have them describe the job Mom and Dad do at home.
- Have them describe the job of someone on television.
- Have them describe the job of someone they see in the workplace.
- Older children should write the job descriptions.

Bizbee Says:

Bee a Self-Employed Costume Designer

- Younger children can talk about the job the sun or the moon does (or a tree, a bee or the rain does).
- Then have the children name any job and list what skills a person would need.
- Who do they know that has those skills?

AGES: 7-18
TIME: 5 minutes per job

AGES: 3-6 can describe things in nature.

MYSTERY SHOPPER
BUSINESS CENTS SKILL #2 RESEARCHING

ACTIVITY:

Have your child select a business which is a competitor to one where someone you know works.

- Pose as a customer and see how you are treated. (This can be over the phone, the internet or in person.)
- Prepare several questions to ask prior to starting. (You can have a complaint, want to return something or have a question that needs to be answered.)
- See how your experience compares to the place where someone you know works.
- Which business needs to improve?

Dr. Cindy Says:

With all of the changes in the economy, even doctors and lawyers need a good business sense to be successful.

AGES: 10-18

TIME: 30+ minutes

CRAZY COPIES
BUSINESS CENTS SKILL #4 IMPLEMENTING

43

ACTIVITY:

Get your children familiar with the use of a copier and fax machine, or faxing from a computer.

- Let them try all settings to see the capabilities.
- Let them send a fax.
- Let them add paper
- Let them make up their own booklet or fax a flyer to their friends.
- Let them handle these items for your needs.

Bizbee Says:

Own a Medical Equipment Company

- Go to an office which provides these services if they are not available directly to you.

AGES: 3-18

TIME: 10 minutes

DESK DRAWER
BUSINESS CENTS SKILL #22 DECISION MAKING

ACTIVITY:

Encourage your children to tackle a desk drawer in need of organization.

- Have them sort and separate.
- Then make a decision on what should stay and what needs to be tossed, or given away.
- Review their choices prior to tossing.
- This exercise can be applied throughout the household and in additional workplace situations.

AGES: 7-18

TIME: 20+ minutes

Dr. Cindy Says:

You will probably be surprised at what your children will say once they start thinking about business. You are creating memories that last forever.

BUSINESS CARD
BUSINESS CENTS SKILL #14 PRESENTING

ACTIVITY:

Suggest that each of your children design their own business card each year.

- This can be done by hand or on the computer.
- Use specialty papers to make the final cards.
- Give them a budget to have duplicated and they can compare various methods.
- Encourage them to design a logo.
- Give them several examples or take them to a printers or an office supply store or internet site to review some ideas.
- They can use at school, with friends, as luggage tags.

Bizbee Says:

Own a Resort

MATERIALS:

- Art Materials
- Specialty Paper

AGES: 5-18   TIME: 30+ min.

POSITIVE THINKING
BUSINESS CENTS SKILL #1 INITIATING

46

ACTIVITY:

Expose your children to the power of positive thinking.

- Let them listen to motivational audio tapes in the car.
- Watch motivational speakers on television.
- Share inspirational sayings and books
- Look to inspirational sites on the internet.
- Introduce them to positive role models.

Dr. Cindy Says:

MATERIALS:

- Inspirational Books and Tapes

Hear what parents say children learn from the Business Cents Method:

- Determination
- Ethics
- Working Together
- Integrity
- Persistence
- Preparation
- Taking Risks
- Enjoying Success
- Control over their life
- Never a Victim ...

AGES: 5-18   **TIME:** 10+ min.

PARTY PLANNER
BUSINESS CENTS SKILL #24 MANAGING

ACTIVITY:

Let children plan family and business get-togethers.

- Let them know the budget and purpose.
- Let them pick a theme and a place.
- Discuss food, favors, time, and day.
- Plan a schedule of activities.
- Let them place the calls to make the arrangements.
- Let them send out the invitations.

Bizbee Says:

Bee a Self-Employed Medical Writer

AGES: 5-18

TIME: 60+ minutes

CLEAN SWEEP
BUSINESS CENTS SKILL #4 IMPLEMENTING

ACTIVITY:

Look at the waste management services of a place where you work. Share what is required with your children.

- Do you use a dumpster?
- Are there any chemical or biohazard wastes which need special handling?
- Does your company recycle?
- Do you use a paper shredder?
- Have them identify several firms which provide such services.
- What are the costs of these services verses services to your home?

AGES: 8-18

TIME: 15 minutes

Dr. Cindy Says:

...Children are learning (Cont.)
- Courage to try new things
- Belief in their abilities
- Freedom
- Humilities over business mistakes
- Continually learning
- Respect for others
- Understanding people
- Thinking
- Passion
- Innovative
- Vision
- Cross Training
- Geography
- Using Technology

INTERNET INVESTIGATION
BUSINESS CENTS SKILL #10 SATISFYING CUSTOMERS

49

ACTIVITY:

Have the children pick three businesses where they have made purchases directly or three products they have purchased through a distributor.

- Find the web site.
- Is it customer friendly?
- Write your comments and suggestions about the site to the President.

- Assess how interested they are in satisfying the customer by the response they get back.

Bizbee Says:

Own an Employment Agency

AGES: 8-18
TIME: 30+ minutes

HOME PAGE
BUSINESS CENTS SKILL #9 COMMUNICATING

50

ACTIVITY:

Encourage your children to look up the home page for a company where one of the family members is employed.

- Is it easy for them to follow?
- Does it take too long?
- Make suggestions on how to improve it.
- If the company does not have one, design one and send the idea to the President.

Dr. Cindy Says:

AGES: 9-18

TIME: 15+ minutes

Research shows that children with a business-owning parent have experiences similar to these, and are most likely to open a business in the future.

VIDEO VIEW
BUSINESS CENTS SKILL #24 MANAGING

51

ACTIVITY:

Let children look at the company video.

- Watch it with them and explain the history of the company and why information was included.
- Tell them how many videos have been sent out and why they are used.
- If your company does not have one, encourage your child to make one of your company or one in the neighborhood.
- Begin by collecting information and writing a script.

Bizbee Says:

*Own a
Sports Team*

- Gain the necessary approvals and do the filming.
- Be sure to present a copy to the President and perhaps tie the project into a school assignment.

MATERIALS:

- Video Camera

AGES: 10-18

TIME: Part 1 – 30 minutes
Part 2 – 120+ minutes

COMPANY HISTORY
BUSINESS CENTS SKILL #2 RESEARCHING

52

ACTIVITY:

Share the history of the company where a family member works or have your child research a company history of interest.

- Begin by listing the sources of information.
- Search for the information and interview any relevant parties.
- Document the history by listing events chronologically.
- Add photos and other information by having them scanned in.
- If there is a business owned by your family, share stories about the early day struggles and how they were overcome.

AGES: 10-18
TIME: 120+ minutes

AGES: 3-9 Share stories

Dr. Cindy Says:

Hear what children say about the Business Cents Method:

- Opportunity to see all sides of a business.
- Time to be with my Dad and Mom
- Learning about value (knew someone had to pay for that)
- Found out how hard it is
- Pride about the work my parents do
- When you're the boss you have security
- I have a new identity

MARKETING MADNESS
BUSINESS CENTS SKILL #14 PRESENTING

53

ACTIVITY:

Encourage the children to keep a "marketing madness" notebook from a business.

- Begin by getting a three-ring notebook.
- Collect any advertising pieces and place in the notebook.
- On each one, mark the date and the place where you saw it.
- They can include pictures of billboards and outdoor advertising, internet sources, and television campaigns.
- This is a good exercise if there is a business in the family.

Bizbee Says:

Bee a
Visiting Nurse

AGES: 9-18

TIME: 10 minutes per advertisement

PHOTO OPPORTUNITY
BUSINESS CENTS SKILL #12 PROMOTING

54

ACTIVITY:

Take a picture of the place where you work and frame it for your child. Encourage them to make a photo album of other businesses.

- They can make a collection of their favorite businesses (for example: restaurants, bike shops, ice cream shops, pizza places).
- Look on the internet to see how photos of businesses are used.
- Look through the advertisements in a Sunday paper for any photos of businesses and how they are used.

Dr. Cindy Says:

Some parents rob their children from "the joy of accomplishment" by giving them too much.

AGES: 8-18
TIME: 10 minutes per photo

AGES: 3-7 Photo of your workplace

CELL PHONE
BUSINESS CENTS SKILL #15 ANALYZING

55

ACTIVITY:

Share your cell phone or telephone bills with your children.

- Let them become familiar with the format of the bill.
- Let them check calls made for accuracy.
- Have the older children call several other phone companies to compare the rate.
- Have them prepare a written analysis for you of costs and benefits.

Bizbee Says:

Own a
Landscaping Business

AGES: 9-18

TIME: 20+ minutes

TRADE SHOW
BUSINESS CENTS SKILL #12 PROMOTING

56

ACTIVITY:

Bring your children along to your next trade show. Spend time with each child.

- Begin by describing the environment and what is expected of them.
- Walk around and observe.
- Let them speak with representatives.
- Look for an opportunity to stay in a booth for a short time and distribute information or freebies.
- Ask them what was their favorite part.
- Have the older children write a report about their experiences.

AGES: 3-9
TIME: 30 min.

AGES: 10-18
TIME: 60+ min.

Dr. Cindy Says:

With financial success, it becomes harder for children to "naturally" learn business sense unless the parents really make an effort to continue these experiences.

PUBLICATION PUNCH
BUSINESS CENTS SKILL #2 RESEARCHING

57

ACTIVITY:

Share your business publications with your children.

- Save and bring them home so they can become familiar with them on a regular basis.
- Go through with the younger ones and discuss any pictures.
- Have the older ones go through and find one thing of interest.

- Discuss what they have found and share with them one point about your industry.

Bizbee Says:

Own a Lumber Mill

AGES:	3-7
TIME:	10 min.
AGES:	8-18
TIME:	15 min.

PURCHASING POWER

Business Cents Skill #16 Purchasing

58

ACTIVITY:

Discuss a purchase you have to make with your child. If you do not have a work example, use a household example.

- Make a list together of what qualities you are looking for.
- Let your child help you think of the different places this item might be available.
- Work with them to gather the information about various choices.
- Let them compare the price, qualities, service, options and timing.
- Ask them which one they would choose.
- Review your decision with them.
- Discuss your purchase six months later. Was it the right choice?

Dr. Cindy Says:

Do not miss your child's school, social, and sports functions. At this time in their lives there is nothing more important. These experiences can never be made up.

AGES: 9-18   **TIME:** 60+ min.

NEW LOCATION

BUSINESS CENTS SKILL #10 Satisfying Customers

59

ACTIVITY:

Relate a business example with your children about expanding locations. If your workplace does not fit this example, use one from the community (for example: a pizza shop, karate studio, tennis shoe shop).

- Do any of the places they regularly go have other locations?

- How should these businesses decide on a new location?

Bizbee Says:

*Make
Sports Equipment*

- What other businesses would you like to see in your community?

- Look for a vacant storeroom and inquire about the rent, amount of space and terms of the lease.

AGES: 9-18

TIME: 20 minutes

BUCK STOPS HERE

BUSINESS CENTS SKILL #22 Decision Making

60

ACTIVITY:

Share a complaint from an employee or customer which you had to solve. Or share a complaint you made to someone.

- Ask your child how they would handle the situation.
- Review the options available and the consequences of each.
- Tell them the results of your experience.
- Let them handle the next complaint either on the giving or receiving end.

AGES: 8-18

TIME: 10+ minutes

Dr. Cindy Says:

Shut off the radio and use time in the car to talk with your child. This is a prime opportunity to engage their interest in business.

Business Cents  **At Play**

Every Saturday night
our family would go out to dinner.
If we would see a dry cleaners
along the way, my father would
always "check it out."
He would ask us to look at the
sign, the neighboring businesses,
and the number of orders on the
rack. He used this information to
find new locations.
To this day I am still sizing up
opportunities.

Chapter 3

TIME TRADE OFF

BUSINESS CENTS SKILL #15 ANALYZING

61

ACTIVITY:

On your next family vacation or business trip, have the children analyze the best way to get there.

- They can compare the price and time to drive verses taking a train or flying or some combination.
- Have them call the airlines or look up the schedules on the internet.
- They can do the same with rental cars and hotels needed.

Bizbee Says:

- Let them write up the options for you.

Own a Trout Farm

AGES: 8-18

TIME: 45 minutes

EXCHANGE GAME
BUSINESS CENTS SKILL #17 ACCOUNTING

62

ACTIVITY:

Encourage the children to plan a trip to another country or to help you with yours.

- Look in the newspaper travel section, on the internet, or call a bank to find out the currency and the exchange rate.

- Give them examples to practice on. (Example: If a shirt costs "x" here then how much would it be there?)

- Find out if there is a service charge to exchange money.

- If you are going to more than one country, have the children calculate if it would be better to first change all into one currency and then to another.

- Teach them how to get a rough exchange in their head (Example: 1.9 to 1 is almost 2 to 1)

Dr. Cindy Says:

Use other Business Cents products such as games, puppets and books to complement and reinforce these activities.

AGES: 9-18   **TIME:** 30+ min.

MAP MANIA
BUSINESS CENTS SKILL #2 RESEARCHING

63

ACTIVITY:

Keep handy a local, state, country and world map. Have your children practice mapping how to most efficiently get around.

- Have them follow a route number and list all of the towns it goes through in both directions from some point.
- Give them two points and ask them to find the quickest way there.
- List natural points along the way such as rivers and mountains.
- List the towns, states, and countries you will be going through on your next trip.
- Have them find the capitals.
- Have them find a country listed in the newspaper each day and locate it on the maps.

Bizbee Says:

*Own a
Recyclying Company*

MATERIALS:

- Local, State, Country, and World Maps

AGES: 3-6 Recognition of the names of towns, states, countries

AGES: 7-18 above activities
TIME: 10+ min. per activity

ITINERARY BUILDING
BUSINESS CENTS SKILL #3 PLANNING

64

ACTIVITY:

Let the children plan your next family vacation.

- Start by deciding on the number of days.
- Allow for travel time and plan how to spend the rest.
- Make a chart with each day listed.
- Then make a list of all of the activities each family member would like to do.
- Try to arrange them in the most efficient way.

Hear the Buzz:

AGES: 5-7 can offer suggestions

TIME: 45+ minutes

AGES: 8-18 can do the planning

A father invited his 7-year-old to accompany him to the office. That night at dinner she asked him what a "resume" was. He wondered where she heard that word. She replied, "your secretary was working on her resume all day today."

TRAVEL BUDGETING
BUSINESS CENTS SKILL #18 FINANCING

65

ACTIVITY:

Once the trip is planned, work back and decide how much it is going to cost. Or start with a budget and plan accordingly along the way.

- List travel
- Hotel
- Local transportation
- Food
- Admissions
- Souvenirs
- Have the children keep track of the expenditures along the way.

Bizbee Says:

**Bee a
Self-Employed Musician**

AGES: 8-18

TIME: 30+ minutes

WARDROBE WIZARD
BUSINESS CENTS SKILL #3 PLANNING

66

ACTIVITY:

Once your trip is planned, it is time to think about packing.

- List shoes and accessories for each activity.
- Consider weather fluctuations and be prepared.
- List all of the other items you may need for various activities.
- Plan for the unexpected.
- Make a list of items which need to be purchased prior to going.

AGES: 5-18

TIME: 45+ minutes

Dr. Cindy Says:

Some of the fondest early experiences remembered by children are regular visits to their parents' job site.

RESERVATIONS CONFIRMED

BUSINESS CENTS SKILL #9 COMMUNICATING

ACTIVITY:

Let the children make the reservations this year.

- Have them write down what they plan to say.
- Contact hotel, airlines, car rentals.
- Keep track of confirmation numbers and details.
- AAA travel booklets and some internet sites are excellent places for children to compare and select hotels and restaurants.

Bizbee Says:

Own a
Dairy Farm

AGES: 8-18

TIME: 30+ minutes

TIME ZONES
BUSINESS CENTS SKILL #15 ANALYZING

ACTIVITY:

Let your children plan a trip to another part of the world.

- Determine the time difference from where you live.
- Use some examples such as, "If you leave at 'x' time, what time will you arrive there?"
- Call the airlines or look on the internet and get the time of departure and the time of arrival for a flight. Determine how long the airplane ride is.
- Ask them to reach a friend in another part of the world at 6 a.m. What time would they have to place the call from their home?

Dr. Cindy Says:

Children gain a sense of pride when they know what their parents do for a living.

MATERIALS:

- Time Zone Chart

AGES: 3-6   **TIME:** 10 Min.

SAFETY SHIPPING
BUSINESS CENTS SKILL #2 RESEARCHING

69

ACTIVITY:

You wish to ship some materials prior to your next trade show or vacation. Let the children determine the best way to ship the goods.

- First identify the ways to get the materials there.
- Make a list of prices and times.
- Consider if you are going to an international destination.
- Discuss the necessary insurance and paperwork
- Do not forget the cost of the packaging materials.

Bizbee Says:

Own an Excavating Company

AGES: 8-18

TIME: 30+ minutes

TRAVEL LOG
BUSINESS CENTS SKILL #4 IMPLEMENTING

ACTIVITY:

Suggest your children document your next vacation.

- Give them (or have them make) a special notebook.
- Bring along markers and pens.
- Let them write the itinerary and experiences along the way.
- They can add their feelings and favorite parts each day.
- Arrange to have them read or share their travel log with an elderly family member of neighbor.

MATERIALS:

- Travel Notebook
- Markers

AGES: 5-18

TIME: 20+min per day

Dr. Cindy Says:

Parents who push their children eliminate the important lesson of trying, failing, struggling, and finally succeeding.

BILLBOARDS GALORE
BUSINESS CENTS SKILL #2 RESEARCHING

71

ACTIVITY:

Encourage your children to open their eyes to billboard and outdoor advertising.

- Have them look for advertisements when in the car.
- What ones do they remember?
- What is their favorite?
- Take note of where the billboards are.
- Make it into a game and keep track on how many billboards are on each side of the road.

Bizbee Says:

Bee a
Self-Employed Geologist

- Have the children also watch for company logos. They get one point for every logo they find.

AGES: 3-7 can count the billboards

AGES: 8-18 to read them
TIME: 5 minutes each

OBSERVE YOUR WORLD
BUSINESS CENTS SKILL #2 RESEARCHING

ACTIVITY:

Teach the children to pay attention to the business world around them.

- Point out factories when driving.
- Take note of business districts and shopping malls.
- Make a list of the businesses there.
- What types of businesses are missing?
- Which businesses are chains?
- Which are independently owned?
- What's the difference?

Dr. Cindy Says:

AGES: 7-18   **TIME:** 15+ min.

AGES: 3-6 can identify
businesses.

Don't call one child your favorite. Treat them all equally.

GROSS VOLUME
BUSINESS CENTS SKILL #18 FINANCING

ACTIVITY:

Let the children try to figure out the Gross Sales Volume of the business.

- Take them to the movies, skiing, or sporting event; ask them to count the number of people there and then multiply it by the ticket price.
- At a motel: Count the number of cars at night and multiply it by the average room rate.
- At an ice cream store: Watch how many cones come out in one hour and multiply it by the price of a cone. Then estimate the number of days open and discount for seasons/weather.

Bizbee Says:

Own a Home and Garden Center

AGES: 10-18

TIME: 45+ minutes

MAKE THE PRODUCT
BUSINESS CENTS SKILL #2 IMPLEMENTING

74

ACTIVITY:

Have the children select several products which they use.

- Make a list of all ingredients or pieces needed.
- What additional supplies would you need?
- What would be the first thing to do in making that product?
- What other steps are needed?
- How long would it take you?
- Let them actually put their planning to use and try it.
- Can you come up with a new twist that might sell?

MATERIALS:

- Based upon the products they choose

AGES: 7-18   **TIME:** 30+ min.

AGES: 3-6 can practice with baking.

Dr. Cindy Says:

Visit our website for updated information.

www.drcindy.com

EVENT EXPENSES
BUSINESS CENTS SKILL #17 ACCOUNTING

75

ACTIVITY:

For those same movies and sporting events in
activity #73, have the children also estimate expenses.

- Make a list of what expenses the business would have.
- Do the same thing for any business you go into.
- Do not forget intangibles like insurance and security.
- Be sure to do this activity if they decide to open any
  of the businesses listed in Chapter 4.
- Make a game and see who has the most items
  on their list.
- Apply the activity to the
  place where you or a family
  member works.

Bizbee Says:

*Own a
Drilling Company*

AGES: 7-18

TIME: 10+ minutes

LESSONS AT LESSONS
BUSINESS CENTS SKILL #19 PROFITING

76

ACTIVITY:

Tell your children to consider anywhere someone in the family goes for classes or lessons as a business.

- What is the gross volume?
- What expenses do they incur?
- How could the business improve?
- How would you describe the business to a friend?
- How does the business attract students?

AGES: 5-18

TIME: 10+ minutes

Dr. Cindy Says:

Children benefit by learning the value of work and the rewards which come with responsibilities.

JINGLE JANGLE
BUSINESS CENTS SKILL #11 ADVERTISING

ACTIVITY:

Ask the children to try to recall a song from a radio or television commercial.

- What product are they trying to sell?
- What are the actual words? (Write to the company if you do not know)
- What type of people would buy the product?
- Think up your own jingle for a product.
  - Try practicing it on a tape recorder.
  - Think up a jingle for the company where you or a family member works.

Bizbee Says:

Make Mining Equipment

AGES: 7-18

TIME: 10+ minutes

RADIO WHAMO
BUSINESS CENTS SKILL #13 SELLING

ACTIVITY:

Occasionally turn the radio on in the car and ask the children to listen to the commercials

- What is the company?
- What are they selling?
- After 5 or 6 commercials, see which one you remember.
- Make up a radio advertisement for the company where you or a family member works.

AGES: 3-18

TIME: 15+ minutes

Hear the Buzz:

A five-year-old recently visited her father's workplace. When the phone rang, she immediately answered it and said, "Daddy Joe's office."

BARBIE THE BUSINESS OWNER
BUSINESS CENTS SKILL #1 INITIATING

79

ACTIVITY:

As your children play with their toys, ask them to think of them as business owners. As the owner of a truck manufacturer, restaurant, doll factory, etc.

- What would they have to do as the owner of ... ?
- What would they have to worry about?
- Who would they need to help them in the business?
- How would they spend their profits?

Bizbee Says:

Own an
Engineering Company

- What expenses would they have to pay?
- What business would they like to own?

MATERIALS:

- General toys

AGES: 3-12   **TIME:** 10+ min.

READING RECORD
BUSINESS CENTS SKILL #1 INITIATING

ACTIVITY:

Share stories with your children about your early days on the job and how others got started.

- Turn your early experiences into exciting, adventurous, age-appropriate stories about the workplace.
- Extend to other people in your family who made a place for themselves.
- Read articles and books and turn them into a version kids would enjoy of others who did the same. (See Chapter Five)
- Tape record each story once you perfected it and make a library of audio tapes.

MATERIALS:
- Books
- Articles
- Tape Recorder

AGES: 3-18   **TIME:** 10 Min.

Dr. Cindy Says:

These 101 ways do not take a lot of money, just time.

VOLUNTEER VALUES
BUSINESS CENTS SKILL #6 TEAMBUILDING

81

ACTIVITY:

Get your children involved in community activities.

- Set up a table at a neighborhood block party.
- Serve at a soup kitchen.
- Donate items to a homeless shelter.
- Help at a community clean up.
- Write your congressman about an issue important to you.

Bizbee Says:

Own a Travel Agency

AGES: 5-18

TIME: 30+ minutes

PROMO PROMOTIONS
BUSINESS CENTS SKILL #12 PROMOTING

82

ACTIVITY:

Encourage your children to recognize promotions used by businesses.

- Have them go through the house and find 3 items with promotions on the label.

- Look for them while shopping.

- Select an item and have them develop a promotion for it.

- Discuss how these promotions affect your buying habits.

AGES: 5-18

TIME: 20+ minutes

Dr. Cindy Says:

If you have an opportunity to only take your child to work with you once a year, do it. Then continue to relate each day to that experience.

COMPANION SALES
BUSINESS CENTS SKILL #13 SELLING

83

ACTIVITY:

Make your children aware of selling items together.

- Play a game and see who can list the most items which can be sold together. (For example: tables & chairs, socks & shoes, airfare & hotels.)
- With every business you visit, ask the children to suggest how they could make companion sales.

Bizbee Says:

*Bee a
Self-Employed Attorney*

AGES: 9-18

TIME: 20+ minutes

BANKRUPT DREAMS
B̲usiness C̲ents S̲kill #2 R̲esearching

84

ACTIVITY:

Make your children aware of businesses which go out of business.

- Look for going-out-of-business signs in your neighborhood. Ask the children "why" the business was closing.
- Look through the newspaper for advertising notices or bankruptcy listings
- Discuss how the business could have avoided the bankruptcy. (Different selection, location, offered better service)
- Discuss the risk of business. In order to get a business they may have pledged their home which could be lost if the business ceases.

  AGES: 9-18

  TIME: 15+ minutes

Dr. Cindy Says:

Be sure stress of the workplace does not get carried home with you. It is the easiest way to make an impression on your children and it will not be good.

ORGANIZATIONAL CHART
BUSINESS CENTS SKILL #5 HIRING

85

ACTIVITY:

Draw the organizational chart illustrating your workplace for your children.

- Have them draw the organizational chart for the family.
- Practice drawing the organizational chart of other families they know.
- Encourage them to ask neighborhood businesses about their organizational chart
- Try to locate organizational charts on the internet.

Bizbee Says:

Own an Ambulance Service

AGES: 7-18

TIME: 20 minutes

BOOK BUSINESSES
BUSINESS CENTS SKILL #7 SUPERVISING

86

ACTIVITY:

When you have several stops to make, let the children decide the most efficient route.

- Give them a list of your stops and let them look at a map or draw one showing the most efficient way.
- Let them supervise you and compare your approach to the one they choose.
- Discuss which is the most efficient choice and why on the way home.

Dr. Cindy Says:

Research shows that the number one thing children 8 to 12 years old want is to be is rich.

MATERIALS:

- Local Map

AGES: 8-18 **TIME:** 10+ min.

COLLECTABLE CATCH
BUSINESS CENTS SKILL #21 NEGOTIATING

87

ACTIVITY:

Consider what type of collection each of your children has. Some are specialized like baseball cards, and dolls, and others are general, such as toys.

- Ask each child to identify his or her favorite item.
- Try to get them to trade that item for something else.
- Do the same with their least favorite item.
- When you ask them to do something, have them put up one of their items as collateral. If they do not complete the task, they have to forfeit the item for a specific time period.

Bizbee Says:

Own a Beauty Salon

AGES: 5-18

TIME: 10 minutes

PET SCHEDULE
BUSINESS CENTS SKILL #24 MANAGING

88

ACTIVITY:

If there is a pet in your household, have the children prepare a care and feeding schedule.

- List all items the dog needs each day of the week.
- Then assign various family members to handle each item.
- Select a manager of the week to oversee the process and pick up if anyone misses their assignment.
- Each manager can decide on consequences of missed assignments.
- Carry the activity over to their own lives. Have them keep a weekly schedule and keep you posted of their needs.

Dr. Cindy Says:

Children today have 10 times as much disposable income as in 1968.

AGES: 5-18

TIME: 15+ minutes

PLAY AROUND
BUSINESS CENTS SKILL #8 EVALUATING

89

ACTIVITY:

Have children introduce themselves and take turns telling a story in front of the room.

- Older children can begin by writing down an opening sentence, key ideas, and the conclusion.
- Younger children can just practice getting up and telling something about their day.
- The audience should do a written evaluation and a yes/no answer to the following: they kept my attention; they spoke clearly; they were easy to follow; I learned something.
- For each yes, the child gets a point and a variety of prizes based on the points

Bizbee Says:

Make Conveyor Belts

AGES: 8-18   **TIME:** 5+ min.

AGES: 3-7

WEEKEND AT GRANDPA'S
BUSINESS CENTS SKILL #2 RESEARCHING

ACTIVITY:

Encourage the children to draw on the business experience of family members and other business owners.

- Have them interview someone about his or her start in Business Cents. Ask them their typical daily schedule.
- These interviews can even be conducted through e-mail.
- Even have them even try to reach someone famous – they might just agree to a few minutes.

AGES: 7-18

TIME: 20+ minutes

Dr. Cindy Says:

Success brings new responsibilities. Teach your children to help others less fortunate along the way.

RATE THE BUSINESS
BUSINESS CENTS SKILL #10 Satisfying Customers

91

ACTIVITY:

Encourage the children to give each business they visit a grade.

- Look at the merchandise selection, customer service, cleanliness, organization and location.
- Size it up and give it a grade from A to F.
- The same activity can also be done on web sites.
- Go back in six months and see the results.

Bizbee Says:

*Own a
Craft Store*

AGES: 5-18

TIME: 20+ minutes

PRICE VALUE
BUSINESS CENTS SKILL #15 ANALYZING

92

ACTIVITY:

Let the children establish a standard shopping list of staples.

- They can go to the store and compare prices on brands.
- Then make up a standard shopping list by brands and just check off each week when needed.
- They can watch the prices over time to see if they fluctuate or if one brand is always cheaper.

Dr. Cindy Says:

The earlier you start the Business Cents Method the easier it is to build a good foundation.

AGES: 8-18

TIME: 45+ mininutes

SIGNS TO FIND
BUSINESS CENTS SKILL #5 HIRING

93

ACTIVITY:

Have children look around the neighborhood business district for help wanted signs in the windows.

- Are any businesses looking for help?
- Ask them where else business owners can find employees.
- Show them the classified ads in the newspaper.
- Have them read them and identify three that look interesting.
- Discuss their choices.
- Also identify job opportunities on the internet.

Bizbee Says:

Own a
Cleaning Service

MATERIALS:

- Classified Ads

AGES: 9-18   **TIME:** 20+ min

FUN FREEBIES
BUSINESS CENTS SKILL #12 PROMOTION

94

ACTIVITY:

Make your children aware of how businesses use special promotions to get them to buy.

- See if they can make a list of promotions businesses use.
- What is their favorite?
- What would be a good promotion for a bank, a restaurant, a travel agency? See how many they can come up with.
- Make a game for them to look through the newspaper or magazines and see how many promotional offers they can find.

Dr. Cindy Says:

After a business experience together consider a treat nearby such as a penny candy after a visit to the printers or a soda pop after visiting the office.

MATERIALS:

- Newspapers
- Magazines

AGES: 3-18   **TIME:** 15+ min.

CUSTOMERS ARE RIGHT
BUSINESS CENTS SKILL #8 EVALUATING

95

ACTIVITY:

After a day of shopping let the children evaluate the customer service.

- Have them think through who was the most helpful.
- Who was the least helpful?
- What could the businesses do to improve customer service?
- What stores would they most likely go back to?
- Apply the same to the internet.
- Share with them the customer service policy where you or a family member works.

Bizbee Says:

Make
Camping Equipment

AGES: 3-18

TIME: 10+ minutes

SELL, SELL, SELL
BUSINESS CENTS SKILL #13 SELLING

ACTIVITY:

Make your children aware of how people are constantly selling around them.

- Watch an infomercial and discuss how they ask for your order.
- What special techniques do they use?
- Look in the yellow pages and see which ads try to get you to take immediate action.
- Play a game by looking at three ads and then trying to recall a phone number. Who made it easy?
- Make up a time sensitive offer for something they would like to sell.

MATERIALS:

- Yellow Pages

Dr. Cindy Says:

Ask a prospective college or trade school for a list of alumni who are entrepreneurs. Interview them to determine the impact of their formal education on their career.

AGES: 8-18   **TIME:** 15+ min.

THE **BIG** PURCHASE
BUSINESS CENTS SKILL #20 INVESTING

97

ACTIVITY:

Explain to your children how to get the most for their money. Prior to a big purchase have them:

- Look in the classified ads and in the yellow pages for a slightly used version.
- Compare against several sources for a new one.
- Offer a 50/50 rule of up to half the price of a new one and encourage them to buy used if available.
- Show them how they can invest their savings.
- Have them consider purchasing products which will help them make money (for example; a bike to make deliveries, a wagon, a computer).

Bizbee Says:

Own a Laundromat

MATERIALS:
- Classified Ads
- Yellow Pages

AGES: 3-6 **TIME:** 10 Min.

AUCTION ACTION
BUSINESS CENTS SKILL #21 NEGOTIATING

98

ACTIVITY:

Save classified ads and let the children look for auctions and flea markets to go to.

- Let them rent a table and make a display of items to sell.
- Let them make a budget for items they are interested in buying.
- Encourage them to ask the price and then offer 20% lower if they are interested.
- Role-play this negotiating process prior to going.
- Tell them to listen to other vendors and buyers first.

MATERIALS:

- Classified Ads

AGES: 3-18   **TIME:** 45+ min.

Dr. Cindy Says:

Parents too can improve their business sense by following the Business Cents Method.

BANK AROUND
BUSINESS CENTS SKILL #20 INVESTING

ACTIVITY:

Encourage the children to shop around for interest rates. Banks are competitive just like other businesses.

- Look in the yellow pages or on the internet for banks nearest you.
- The children can call and ask about the various rates they offer.
- They should keep a chart with the names of the bank down the left side and the products across the right.
- The different rates can then be easily filled in.

Bizbee Says:

Own a Video Production Company

- Be sure to ask about penalties for early withdrawals.
- Encourage the children to open a bank account, make regular deposits even if small and move up into certificates of deposit.

MATERIALS:

- Yellow Pages

AGES: 5-18 **TIME:** 20+ min.

TEAM PURCHASE
BUSINESS CENTS SKILL #6 TEAMWORK

100

ACTIVITY:

Enable your children to better work together by having them make joint purchases.

- Play the money game by giving them a sack of money (your loose change) and letting them decide as a group on some purchase such as ice cream or a special treat.
- Let them rotate being the leader and managing the process.
- Have them decide on how to make the decision: unanimous, consensus, leader picks, or some other method.

MATERIALS:

- Sack of Change

Dr. Cindy Says:

Ability is what you are capable of doing.

Motivation determines what you do.

Attitude determines how well you do it.

Lou Holtz

AGES: 3-18   **TIME:** 15 min.

CHANGE BACK
BUSINESS CENTS SKILL #17 ACCOUNTING

101

ACTIVITY:

With every opportunity when using cash to make purchases, let the children pay the bill and get the change back.

- Be sure they count the change.
- Let them calculate the tip in restaurants.
- Have them add up the bill in their head to double check.
- Let them calculate the tax.

Bizbee Says:

Bee a Self-Employed Developer

AGES: 8-18 **TIME:** 5 min.

AGES: 3-7 can pay the bill

Practice Makes Perfect

Every summer as a pre-teen I would look forward to Jacobs Flea Market. My mother would let me rent a table and gather up household items and clothing to sell. I bargained with customers, overheard the other vendors, and recorded my sales each week. It was terrific to make a record sales day and then decide what to do with my earnings after paying the expense for the table.

Chapter 4

Practice Makes Perfect

One of the best ways to reinforce these skills is through actually applying them in a business. Early in life the risks are smaller and there is time to learn from one's mistakes

Some parents who own larger businesses have started new

At Home
In and around the neighborhood

Arrange a BLOCK PARTY. Make a schedule, get neighbors involved, and calculate a small fee per person for your efforts in running the program.

Set up a BABYSITTING REFERRAL SERVICE. Line up a solid staff, introduce yourself to area neighbors, develop a good telephone message system.

Provide a SERVICE COLLECTING equipment, clothes, things from your neighbors. Visit on a regular basis. Negotiate a percent if you handle large items. Find outlets to sell the items.

Offer an IN AND OUT, UP AND DOWN SERVICE. Each week take garbage cans out to the curb and the next day bring the cans in. Expand your services to include holiday decorations.

small enterprises for the primary purpose of letting the children have an actual experience. One father organized his nine young children and gave them a small amount of money to begin investing in real estate. Today the company has grown so large that several of the children are employed there.

Here are a few new spins to low cost businesses

AT WORK

PLANT FLOWERS at local businesses by working with the Chamber of Commerce. Place pots outside and don't forget a contract to keep them watered.

Host a regular BREAKFAST/BAKE SALE STAND in an office building or area that doesn't already have service.

Conduct INTERNET RESEARCH for small businesses who might not have the time to do so.

Co-ordinate CAR WASHING at an office building or restaurant. Sell tickets as people drive into work and wash them while they are inside.

Work with a local DRY CLEANER for a discount if you PICK UP AND DELIVER the clothes. Find customers at office buildings, schools, businesses and make a schedule.

Go to a personal care home and offer COMPANION SERVICES to the patients. Sit, read, entertain, talk on a regular basis.

pre-teens and teens can operate. Younger children should be encouraged to play a role as well. Go through each of the 101 ways to give children Business Cents and relate the activity to a business your child is interested in. Additional references on actually operating a small business are listed in the following chapter.

AT PLAY

Start a PEN PAL SERVICE. Offer grandparents something nice to do by having you write to their grandchildren once a month for a year.

Start a BEVERAGE AND SNACK CONCESSION anyplace children come on a weekly basis for lessons.

Be creative. MAKE SOMETHING ORIGINAL and sell it at craft shows.

If you are good at a sport or skill, OFFER WEEKLY LESSONS.

If you are artistic, MAKE PERSONALIZED GREETING CARDS. Sell them with a portfolio.

Take a BOOTH AT THE FAIR. Offer face painting, children's activities.

Resources

I grew up hearing stories about my great grandmother in Italy who developed business sense out of necessity. She was a young widow with eleven children. As the story goes, she trapped small animals in the forest and walked down the mountain to trade them for vegetables and fruits at the local market. Stories about my grandmother were added to this collection as she raised chickens and fruits. The city dwellers would take a train to the country and she set up a stand to sell eggs and homemade jams. Today there are numerous resources available for you to use to inspire your children.

Chapter 5

The Fortunate Fortunes
Nathan Aaseng
Lerner Publications
75 Pages – 1989
Success stories of entrepreneurs who used their imagination.

From Rags to Riches
People who Started Businesses from Scratch
Nathan Aaseng
Lerner Publications
1990
Stories of the beginning of Apple Computers, Sears, Wall Street Journal, J.C. Penny, Hershey's Chocolate, and Ebony Magazine.

The Problem Solvers
Nathan Aaseng
Lerner Publications
80 Pages – 1989
Describes individuals with insight and curiosity who formed successful companies by finding creative solutions to problems.

The Rejects
Nathan Aaseng
Lerner Publications
80 Pages – 1989
Describes various companies that succeeded despite initial rejection by experts.

Fast Cash for Kids
Bonnie and Noel Drew
Career Press
250 Pages – 1995
Packed with terrific money making ideas.

Towards Togetherness, The Cooperative Games, Songs and Activities Handbook
Richard Burrill
The Anthro Company, PO Box 661765, Sacramento, CA 95866, (916) 971-1675
110 Pages – 1994
This book teaches children teamwork and self-worth through the American Indian philosophy of living. Through the use of games, children come to understand how important it is to respect one another via cooperation.

Rowena & The Wonderful Jam and Jelly Factory
Rowena JAAP
Stanley Press, Inc., PO Box 11107, Norfolk, VA 23517
30 Pages – 1987
A child's story about turning a closed business into a magical operating factory.

Lifestyle Math
Mindy Bingham, Jo Willhite and Shirley Myers
Academic Innovations, 3463 State St., Suite 219A, Santa Barbara, CA 93105, (805) 967-8015
112 Pages – 1994
Through a series of worksheets, the reader is able to determine and budget a lifestyle based on career choices.

The Monster Money Book
Loreen Leedy
Holiday House
28 Pages - 1992
This book uses a whimsical story to assist children in understanding how to budget money, sell products, and how dues are used when belonging to a club.

A Fortune Branches Out
Margaret Mahy
Delacorte
83 Pages - 1994
Tessa Fortune and her cousins want to raise one hundred dollars for the New Zealand National Telethon but when their plans begin to falter, Tessa learns some valuable lessons about her goal of becoming a rich executive.

Mama Bear
Chyng Feng Sun
Houghton Mifflin Co.
1994
When Mei-Mei fails in her attempt to earn money by selling cookies her mother helps her see a special gift she has had all along.

Better Mousetraps...Product Improvements that Lead to Success
Nathan Aaseng
Lerner Publications
80 Pages - 1990
Brief biographies of individuals who improved, refined, and perfected various products and processes.

If You Made a Million
David M. Schwartz
Lothrope, Lee & Shepard Books
44 Pages - 1989
This charming story helps children convert numbers into monetary values.

Money-Book Store Catalog
National Center for Financial Education, PO Box 34070, San Diego, CA 92163-4070, (619) 232-8811
1995

Bringing Up Parents
Alex J. Packer, Ph.D.
Free Spirit Publishing - To Order: 1-800-440-4003
264 Pages - 1993
Illustrated ways teenagers can improve their relationship with their parents through mutual trust and respect.

Jomo and Mats
Alyssa Chase
Marsh Media, PO Box 8082, Shawnee Mission, KS 66208
31 Pages - 1993
When the riverbed dries up, Jomo the elephant learns that digging a well is more important than outdoing his brother.

Career Choices
Mindy Bingham and Sandy Stryker
Academic Innovations, 3463 State St., Suite 219A, Santa Barbara, CA 93105, (805) 967-8015
288 Pages - 1993
A guide for teens and young adults to help them identify who they are and what their professional future holds.

Business
Janet Cook
Usborne
48 Pages – 1985
Packed with how-to advice on operating a business.

Girls and Young Women Inventing
Frances Karnes, Ph.D. and Suzanne Bean, Ph.D.
Free Spirit Publishing
168 Pages – 1995
Experiences of girls actually working with their inventions.

The Golden Atlas for Children
Neil Morris
Western Publishing
46 Pages – 1994
Illustrates what products come from each region or country around the world.

The National Directory of Internships
The National Society for Experimental Education
673 Pages – 1995
Description of thousands of internship opportunities listed by location and field of interest.

Work, Study Travel Abroad
Council on International Educational Exchange
St. Martin's Press
500 Pages
Hundreds of opportunities for an international experience.

Bring More

To Your Family, School & Community

BUSINESS CENTS PROGRAMS:
Now available for your community

⬡ **CAMP BUSINESS CENTS**   Weekly summer program (Ages 3-15)

⬡ **BUSINESS CENTS ACADEMY**   Year-round business lessons delivered on a weekly basis for preschool, elementary, junior high, and high school levels.

BUSINESS CENTS PRODUCTS

⬡ **ABC's OF BUSINESS**   Activities Book (Ages 5-14)

⬡ **BUSINESS CENTS**   "The friends & family, feelings and
finance Board Game" 2-8 players
(All Ages)

⬡ **BIZBEE THE PUPPET**   (Ages Infant-8)

⬡ **PLAY BUSINESS BAG**   Everything needed to play the
business owner (Ages 3-12)

⬡ **BUZZ AWAY** Card Game   48 Business Owner Cards for 1-6
Players, (Ages 3-18)

⬡ **BUSINESS CAN BE FUN KITS**   (Ages 7-18)

- Marketing Magic
- Create a Product

⬡ **BUSINESS CENTS CURRICULUM GUIDES**
Available for each of the five skill sets

- Book 1 – Ages 3-6   Preschool
- Book 2 – Ages 7-10 Elementary
- Book 3 – Ages 11-14 Junior High
- Book 4 – Ages 15-18 Senior High

⬡ **HONEY MONEY**   Television and Video Series Coming
Soon. To order contact:

BUSINESS CENTS RESOURCES
3038 Washington Pike
Bridgeville, PA 15017
1-800-67-CINDY or 412-221-8924
Fax No. 412-221-0150
WWW.DRCINDY.COM

ADVISING SERVICES FOR BUSINESS OWNERS AND THEIR FAMILIES

◇ Dr. Cindy works with individual families using the *"Business Cents Guide to Operating a Business with Your Family: 12 Steps to Govern Yourselves Through the Generations"*.

KEYNOTE SPEECHES AND WORKSHOPS

⬡ Dr. Cindy brings Business Cents to trade groups, associations, and organizations around the world.

MEET DR. CINDY

Dr. Cindy Iannarelli is the nation's leading expert on business skill training for children. Dr. Cindy brings first-hand experience to her work as an entrepreneur herself. She stepped in to manage the family enterprises at age twenty due to her father's untimely death. Today she is one of three generations in the family businesses. This real world experience combined with academic research is the foundation of her company, Business Cents Resources.

Dr. Cindy is the founder and director of the Center for Family Business at Indiana University of Pennsylvania and she teaches at The University of Pennsylvania's Wharton Program for Family Controlled Corporations. She has an MBA and Ph.D. from the University of Pittsburgh School of Business. Dr. Cindy maintains dual citizenship with Italy and addresses audiences worldwide.

INDEX

AGES	ACTIVITY NUMBERS
3 & up	1, 4, 5, 7, 14, 25, 27, 31, 32, 34, 43, 56, 57, 71, 72, 78, 79, 80, 94, 95, 97, 98, 100, 101
5 & up	11, 19, 20, 21, 23, 26, 29, 36, 45, 46, 47, 66, 70, 76, 77, 81, 82, 87, 88, 91, 99
7 & up	2, 3, 6, 9, 10, 12, 13, 17, 18, 22, 24, 33, 35, 37, 41, 44, 63, 74, 75, 85, 90
8 & up	15, 16, 30, 39, 40, 48, 49, 54, 60, 61, 64, 65, 67, 69, 86, 89, 92, 96
9 & up	8, 28, 42, 50, 51, 52, 53, 55, 58, 59, 62, 68, 73, 83, 84, 93
12 & up	38

You are on Your Way to Making

Business Cents

Common Sense in Your Family